Dermatillomania Treatment and Self-Help

How to Stop Chronic, Obsessive Compulsive Skin Picking

by Jonathan Cross

Table of Contents

Introduction 1

Chapter 1: Understanding Dermatillomania 7

Chapter 2: Identifying Stressful Triggers 13

Chapter 3: Botanical Miracles to Include in Your Routine 19

Chapter 4: A Drastic But Highly Effective Tactic ... 25

Chapter 5: Employing Diversionary Tactics 29

Conclusion 35

Introduction

For some odd reason, the world at large seems to think that sufferers of dermatillomania — compulsive skin picking — do so out of a weird urge for attention. Well, that couldn't be further from the truth. Having seen someone close to me suffer through the clenches of this disorder, I can attest to the fact that this behavior is not a mere choice — it's an all-pervasive disease. Not only are sufferers *not* trying to seek attention, they go to great lengths to ensure that they receive as little attention as possible, no thanks to the guilt and society-imposed shame that they feel as a response to their illness.

Dermatillomania, or compulsive skin picking, is usually caused by some sort of stress that leads to picking as an emotional outlet, the results of which bring on additional stress, which only causes more picking. It becomes a vicious cycle that's so all-encompassing that many sufferers feel trapped without a way out, all the while feeling insecure and judged by those around them.

Well, at least one reprieve from this nightmarish situation is that this disorder has *finally* been recognized by mental health professionals as an illness in its own right, and not just a lowly symptom. The downside though, is that the world has yet to truly understand the nature of this behavior as much as other more "famous" diseases like Schizophrenia and Dementia. The proof in the pudding is in the fact that most sufferers get advice along the lines of "You can stop if you really want," or "Yeah, I used to cut myself to feel good too" when they attempt to share their pain with others.

Let's get one thing clear – there's nothing good about the fact that many sufferers zone out and by the time they return to the present moment, they've added another oozing, bleeding scab to the plethora adorning every conceivable inch of their body. But, the good news is this: Dermatillomania *can* be stopped. Of course, if you have the time and the financial means, seeking professional psychological therapy is an effective way of overcoming dermatillomania. However, if you prefer to battle the affliction on your own, then this book will arm you with all the tools you need.

In this book, you'll be provided with a mixture of psychological techniques that will teach you how to channel the urge to pick, catch yourself in the act, and even tone it down gradually until it no longer has a death grip on your mind or occurs subconsciously without your approval. None of these methods require any medication: the only thing they require from you is a genuine desire to dig your way out of the clutches of this dermatillomania.

© Copyright 2015 by Miafn LLC - All rights reserved.

This document is geared towards providing reliable information in regards to the topic and issue covered. The publication is sold with the idea that the publisher is not required to render accounting, officially permitted, or otherwise, qualified services. If advice is necessary, legal or professional, a practiced individual in the profession should be ordered.

- From a Declaration of Principles which was accepted and approved equally by a Committee of the American Bar Association and a Committee of Publishers and Associations.

In no way is it legal to reproduce, duplicate, or transmit any part of this document in either electronic means or in printed format. Recording of this publication is strictly prohibited and any storage of this document is not allowed unless with written permission from the publisher. All rights reserved.

The information provided herein is stated to be truthful and consistent, in that any liability, in terms of inattention or otherwise, by any usage or abuse of any policies, processes, or directions contained within is solely and completely the responsibility of the recipient reader. Under no circumstances will any legal responsibility or blame be held against the publisher for any reparation, damages, or monetary loss due to the information herein, either directly or indirectly.

Respective authors own all copyrights not held by the publisher.

The information herein is offered for informational purposes solely, and is universal as so. The presentation of the information is without contract or any type of guarantee assurance.

The trademarks that are used are without any consent, and the publication of the trademark is without permission or backing by the trademark owner. All trademarks and brands within this book are for clarifying purposes only and are the owned by the owners themselves, not affiliated with this document.

Chapter 1: Understanding Dermatillomania

Recently recognized under the term "Excoriation Disorder" (ED), dermatillomania is a disorder which has yet to be understood or addressed with any specificity by the world of mental health professionals. Not just that, but chronic sufferers of this affliction are also often deeply misunderstood by the lay world at large. With that in mind, let's clear the air and try to define vague parameters to this disease which in itself encompasses a dizzying array of behaviors and symptoms.

To begin with, dermatillomania is *not* a symptom of other mental disorders, though it does accompany some at times. The sufferers of this horrendous condition, on its own demerits, go through tremendous pain and anxiety which often leaves them with severe physical and mental scarring.

Although this disorder sometimes starts as an accompaniment to underlying skin disorders, more often than not, sufferers start along this path as a nervous tic or stress-induced repetitive behavior. It is not true that all those inflicted with ED began picking on their skin because they hated themselves. ED sufferers are often quite comfortable in their own skin before the onset of this disease. It's only later, once the scars and related damage which comes hand-in-hand with ED start showing up quite prominently, that it starts taking a toll on their self-esteem and self-image. Many people simply started popping pimples or messing around with perceived imperfections in order to accentuate perfectly good skin.

When an ED "attack" (for want of a better word) is triggered, sufferers are often alone and they zone out while they're picking at themselves. The feeling, for some people, is like an itch that can't be ignored or a mission which needs to be accomplished if all is to be right once again within their world. The particularly dangerous part here for the sufferers is that some zone out enough to do damage to muscles and other underlying tissues before they come out of their daze—and these are documented instances. For those who don't "check out" from conscious activity quite so strongly, they're still left with several bleeding scabs all over their back, chest, feet, arms, legs, face, and scalp—pretty much any spot which can be conveniently reached while in a standing, sitting, or lying position. These particular scabs, especially since each sufferer has a few stress spots or favorites, never even get the chance to heal to a scar for weeks, months, or years in some cases.

Every sufferer has ED triggers, essentially scenarios, stimuli, thoughts, or actions which are extremely stress-inducing. Each time a trigger comes up, the intensity of the next attack may vary based on the strength of a particular trigger, and yet the sufferer zones out at the next available chance nonetheless. Once an ED attack is triggered, the impulse to get lost in picking at your own skin becomes so strong that ignoring it only adds to the massive stress, which further reinforces the need to either pluck at a scab or create a new wound.

Apart from the psychological damage caused by watching the body slowly become covered with open or semi-healing wounds, the sufferers open themselves up to septicemia along with a whole host of bacterial infections. This can be particularly life threatening if the sufferer is pregnant, had recent surgeries, or was exposed to medicine-resistant strains of microbes.

No-one, and I mean absolutely no one, outside of people suffering from obsessive compulsive disorders (to which this disorder has been officially related) can truly understand the impact and cost brought by the illness onto its sufferers. This makes healthy processing of mental tribulations, which are part and parcel of everyday life, highly difficult. Moreover, the guilt created by the damage they themselves have wrought on their body complicates intimate relations in twisted ways.

Although I hardly need to tell you all of this, seeing as it's highly probable that if you're reading this book, you're suffering from the same thing—this chapter is aimed towards those around you rather than at you, in the hopes that better understanding the truth of your anguish from an objective outsider, may help secure the support and nurturing environment that many aren't lucky enough to receive, before they attempt to combat their very mind to overcome ED.

So, for all of you who came here looking for an answer—let's move on from all the doom and gloom, and get you suited up for the big fight.

Chapter 2: Identifying Stressful Triggers

The first thing any general worth his stars would tell you is—know thine foe. However, being a psychological disorder, the hardest part to contend with in this situation is that the foe *is you*—or more specifically, your own head. Now, that doesn't mean that you can't win. After all, even the late John Nash, Jr. battled with his schizophrenia every day and still managed to win himself a Nobel Prize, and went on to receive an Abel Prize just days before his tragic death in 2015. What it *does* mean though is that the time to sit and fret over your situation is over. The time for action is nigh.

Till this point, while you've had a vague idea of the larger stresses and patterns of picking that define your own experience with ED, the finer points have always been lost in a haze. Well, bucko, vagueness is the enemy of strategy. Imagine how D-Day would have gone had the American battle tacticians been pointed due east by the spies and informed that the enemy is "somewhere over there."

So, pick up a tiny booklet or a smartphone—anything you can carry around with you at all times really—and start paying attention. Although I'm entirely sure you're quite aware of how much you pick, I doubt you understand with any accuracy *exactly* how much you pick. Also, if the thought of finding that out scares you in even the slightest—you need to go through this exercise more than anyone else. If you ever wish to overcome ED in any significant form, you'll have plenty of fears which you'll need to face—of which this will probably be the most basic.

Whenever you encounter a stressful situation, pay greater attention to determine what your particular "tug" to start picking feels like. Though many among you will already be aware of it, plenty more won't and will often answer the need without paying any particular attention to the call. Once you're aware of how that tug feels to you, you'll be prepared to go on your guard rather than space out and submit to the urge.

In your chosen way to document all of it, note down each time in the day when you feel the tug to pick surface up. Along with that, if you suspect having some favorite spots in different situations and yet can't consciously differentiate between them, write down the spot you chose to pick as well as the position your body was in at that point. Also, make sure that you list out the exact source of your stress—for example, if you feel that tug during some conversations but not all the time, the partner isn't the source of your stress as much as the topic of the conversation. You'll also be able to start differentiating between periods when that tug is stronger and when it's weaker—which will often say just as much about your vulnerability at different points of time in the day as it will about the relevance to stress of that specific trigger. You may be far more exhausted at the end of a day than the middle of it, and so more susceptible to picking even when faced with less stressful triggers.

Therefore, through this comprehensive exercise, not only will you manage to pinpoint your specific sources of stress, but also how important they may be on the list of stresses for you. Furthermore, it will allow you to sketch out plans of the day based on the times which you recognize as causing greater vulnerability. As an example, if you eat heavier lunches and get drowsy which then leads to more picking, you can try switching to lighter meals and check if that reduces your picking behavior during that time every day. If you feel like studies and exams overly stress you out, and you keep picking at that spot on your arm or thigh in response, try walking around while studying in an effort to fight the urge.

See? I told you detailed information comes in handy. The biggest problem which comes up when we talk about illnesses is that people automatically assume that they follow similar patterns of progression and exhibit similar behavioral symptoms—though nothing is further from the truth, especially in psychological disorders. And so, if you want to come up with a game plan which is specifically tailored to answering your individual needs, you need to draw up a battle map using information relevant to your own battlefield—and not one which would pertain to wars fought three continents away or four centuries ago.

One more bit of information which you might want to know is that for many people, being presented with reasonably incontrovertible proof of the depth of their disorder can be a difficult experience to navigate. So, if you start feeling lost, always remember that nothing can harm you—it was there regardless of whether you knew about it or not. The question then becomes—if you have an insatiable enemy come what may, would you rather be pudgy, ignorant, and caught with your pants down behind the bushes, or with a kickass weapon and ten years worth of experience as a highly decorated soldier? I think the answer is rather obvious—neither, really. You would want to be the military genius who understands his enemy's every move, and makes an effective trap from some wood chips and half a Snickers bar.

Chapter 3: Botanical Miracles to Include in Your Routine

Now that we've effectively started compiling data on your disorder and you're already attempting to recognize and respond to visible patterns in your behavior, it's time to draw up battle tactics. However, before we do so, there's a simple truth which you must recognize—no single form of treatment is ever entirely effective in isolation. Therefore, what we're going to try from this point onwards are broad battle tactics which are designed to answer as many individual needs as possible among all of you out there. Though I'll provide broad baselines on how each tactic works, they will all have to be individually tailored to your needs depending on when you believe your urges to be at their strongest. Well, that's exactly why you went through all the trouble of documenting your experience to begin with—so it's a good thing you came well prepared to the fight.

One of the primary problems faced by many ED sufferers is their constant complaint and sense of dissatisfaction with their skin overall. Even though this disorder may have started for you as a way to crush imperfections and get gorgeous skin, it twisted somewhere along the way, and the result has left you far unhappier than before. Now, for people with skin-related urges, the tug comes from various sources—if their skin feels too oily or sticky, too dry or rough, too dirty or sweaty after a long day of work, or covered in too many pimples and blackheads. Regardless, the facial skin in particular becomes a large source of stressful triggers, and so picking at your perceived imperfections becomes the first order of business as soon as you're confidently able to do so without interruptions.

Therefore, your first move in the battle should be to initiate a proper skin-cleansing routine especially before bed or right after returning home, if you've identified these as particularly stressful times. Again, don't use store-bought face packs or cleansers. Instead, use various ingredients found in your own kitchen to make great packs.

The first one would be the leaves of the Indian Lilac or the Nimtree. Though this may be a slightly more exotic find, the leaves of this particular botanical miracle have long been touted for their great soothing and antibacterial prowess. If you can get your hands on some of these, all you need to do is to slow boil them for half an hour to forty minutes on a low flame, and then directly apply the water to your face, arms, legs, and any other place where your skin irritates you and leads you to pick at it. Wash it off after roughly an hour. Not only will this effectively keep your scabs clean and disinfected, but also give you soft, glowing skin and relative freedom from pimples and blackheads.

The next ingredient would be honey. Greatly acclaimed for its soothing feeling, some honey mixed in equal parts with milk makes a great face pack for daily or twice-weekly skin softening and cleaning. The third suggestion would be coarsely ground coffee beans, not powder, with milk. This particular combination works as a great scrub to get off that pesky feeling of having something on your face, while softening the skin and any scabs so that they stretch or tear less on their own. However, whether or not it's an effective face wash for you depends on the severity of your ED. For those with severe afflictions, the scrubbing action of the coffee may incite more skin picking and cause more damage than reduce it.

Another suggestion to help with this problem is to use Vitamin E oils. Easily available at the market, Vitamin E oils are amazing at giving suppleness and elasticity to your skin. Moreover, they're awesome at helping cuts and wounds heal well, and prevent dry scabs from breaking open on their own. Plus, since they're quite slippery, they prevent you from effectively picking at your wounds and scabs.

The last suggestion in this chapter is a mixture of honey and mustard. Since mustard is an amazing antibacterial agent, and honey works great at soothing and softening your skin, this is a particularly effective combination if it's followed by a face wash which you *know* helps your skin feel better. One point to keep in mind here is that mustard can stain your face yellow, and this may persist for a few hours—so attempt this only when you know you don't have any social obligations to fulfill.

There are literally hundreds of other ingredients which you can commonly find around your kitchen, and any combination of them can make your skin feel amazing. As long as you find the combination that's right for you, this routine—supplemented by a simple facial wash on days when you don't have time to be more fancy or creative—will leave you feeling better about your skin and less likely to get the urge to start picking as soon as you're home. However, if you're still hard pressed for time, or usually encounter these urges associated with the feel of your skin while you're outside, start carrying packs of wet wipes with you. Many of these are readily available with some form of antibacterial or cleansing agents, and you can comfortably pick scents which suit your sense of aesthetics.

Chapter 4: A Drastic But Highly Effective Tactic

For those of you suffering from ED, the subject of this topic is rather obvious. Mirrors. Often a great source of anxiety, a mirror plays a large part in the lives of many people afflicted with ED. In fact, most of those suffering from this condition started on their journey with this disorder by standing in front of mirrors and picking at tiny, perceived imperfections in their skin. Moreover, the urge to pick for many *EDers* comes from the stress caused by seeing their reflection—scabs and scars and all—reflected in mirrors.

So, how do we resolve this problem? Easily enough as it turns out. Make it quite a chore to get to a mirror. While this may seem weirdly counter-intuitive, mirrors aren't as indispensable a part of everyday life as everyone assumes them to be. For example, if you're inclined to carrying wet wipes with you (among all the suggestions outlined in the previous chapter), you can easily clean your face through the sense of touch alone without having to look in a mirror to do so.

Therefore, get rid of any unnecessary mirrors around the house. While you're at it, shift any mirrors which are easily visible from your usual seating spots. Relocate any mirrors in your bedroom or living room to inconvenient corners, and angle them away so that you would actively have to be standing in uncomfortable positions to look at them if need be.

If you have any particular mirrors in your bathroom which you can't get rid of, cover them with a towel, plastic, or sheet of paper so that you would have to first uncover it if you wish to see your own reflection. As much as possible, also avoid the urge to check yourself in reflective surfaces at stores and other public places if you have no direct need (such as checking the fit of a particular piece of clothing on yourself) to do so.

I need to make it clear that undertaking this step doesn't mean that you're afraid of what you'll see or that you should be afraid of your own reflection—but heroin addicts aren't rehabilitated by hanging bags of heroin around them just to see if they're up for the challenge. There will come a day when these steps will no longer be required. But till then, do yourself a favor and remove any unnecessary stress which may induce further attacks. You're not running away from anything by taking this step, but rather allowing your strength to recharge before you take on the hardest part of this fight.

Chapter 5: Employing Diversionary Tactics

One thing that every EDer understands well is that this disease isn't a switch which can be flipped on and off. You can't just wake up one day and, just because you feel like it, *stop* doing it even if in the midst of its iron grip. However, the one thing you *can* do is to fool the disease. Employ diversionary tactics, and channel the urge elsewhere. And that's precisely what we're going to discuss in this chapter.

There are a few ways in which you can employ diversionary methods to control the affliction, if not eradicate it altogether. The first one is to use puppets and toys. Well, if that sounds so strange to you—it won't soon enough. However, before we get on with this step, the very first thing which you need to do is to lock away your picking tools in a drawer or a cabinet—nail clippers, files, and anything else you've ever used to pick and scratch your skin. This works better if you make it particularly inconvenient to get up and take them out. Before you start getting too anxious, I'm not telling you to throw them out or even throw away the key after you've locked everything up. All you're doing is making matters just enough of a hassle and a bother that the decision to take something from that collection becomes a conscious decision rather than the execution of a random, meandering thought.

Getting back to the point, the biggest problem with keeping checks on this affliction is the simplicity in the way it works. You feel the urge, almost like an itch, and so you absent-mindedly scratch it. However, since it makes you feel less stressed and helps you cope with other stuff, you keep scratching it. Gradually, you zone out while you're still picking and scratching, and before you know it—you've picked it into an open wound. Now, depending on the pattern of your own disease, the next time you feel the urge, you're either going to head for a new spot if it can be conveniently reached or you're going to go for the same old spot if it's slightly scabbed over—since that weirdly gives more satisfaction. Chances are that if you've dealt with ED for a while, you'll have some favorite spots depending on how you sit or lie down in bed.

Whatever the case may be, the simplest truth here is that your hands cause this damage by listening to your brain instead of your will—and I'm sure that you of all people will understand exactly what I mean. Therefore, the easiest way (loosely speaking) is to keep your hands busy whenever you get the urge. This way, instead of having to deal with an active urge with empty hands as soon as you encounter it, your brain will have to contend with conscious activity which will allow you to keep pushing the promised time when you intend to give in further and further. Most EDers have experienced that if you fight the urge for the first twenty minutes to half an hour of its occurrence, the desperate need to give in or the unconscious submission after zoning out is greatly reduced.

So, since you've already identified the times and causes which trigger the urge to pick the strongest, the first thing which you're going to do is leave yourself reminders to not give in. Whichever times in the day that you've identified as the periods with greatest picking activity, set alarms and memos on your phone to remind yourself to fight the urge and not submit to the disease. Whenever you can, remind yourself that you look amazing and that you're better than being chained to this affliction. While these will not work by themselves, they will form the foundation upon which you can weave your network of diversions.

The next thing you do is go out and buy yourself some cute finger puppets—about six of them to be exact. Cheap, cute, and fun, they provide the best answer to this particular problem without hampering yourself. Since most people mainly pick at their skin using their thumbs, index, and middle fingers at the most, these are the fingers on which you'll wear the puppets and leave them on whenever you can. Whenever you feel the urge to start scratching or picking, the feel of the finger puppets will remind you not to give in to the urge to pick, and thus help you jolt yourself out of the absentminded urge and get back to the present.

If these don't work, and you've been attempting to utilize them while you're by yourself—you can also use gloves and oven mitts to do the same job. The point to take away from here is that your affliction constantly keeps trying to fool you into following this damaging pattern of behavior. Instead, you need to set up mental roadblocks in such a manner than you would need to consciously choose to ignore every one of them in order to pick at your skin.

Another method which you can use is to either employ fidgety hobbies or, as an alternative, "fidgeting toys." These are largely mechanical answers to the problem where, instead of blocking your way to be able to pick with any satisfaction, you will either keep your hands busy through mechanical and time-consuming hobbies or you will keep toys and such around which you can pick up and play with if you ever need to keep your hands full. Although knitting and model-making serve as effective examples for fidgety hobbies, literally anything could be used as fidgeting toys. These include items as simple, yet ultimately effective, as bubble wrap.

However, there will always be times when you're either in social groups or among people in front of whom it wouldn't be possible to satisfy your itch. In such cases, the best way to find a way through the affliction is to clench your fingers into a fist and breathe your way through it. Though this particular option may take some time before it's entirely effective, it becomes important after consecutively practicing it across different stressful situations and triggers.

Conclusion

This short book's goal is to open your eyes to the various possibilities by which you can retain a measure of peace and start working your way out of the torture rack of ED. Although the situation is difficult, it's never hopeless as long as you're willing to fight it with all the will power you've got.

That being said, you'll notice that there's a conspicuous lack of medication-talk in this book. This was intentional, primarily carried out to emphasize the fact that even if the book pointed out excellent techniques to reduce your mental load, there's a real need for healthcare management by professionals. While the techniques in this book will help you reduce the need to scratch and pick to a point where you feel you may make a conscious choice, the psychological healthcare personnel will be responsible for helping you address the very root of the problem—the mental triggers. The steps outlined in this guide will help wean you off the need to pick at your skin. The next steps which you can take—guided by a psychologist—help your mind to deactivate stress triggers and render them permanently impotent. This logical next move ensures that you don't have to go through the rest of your life like a junkie—always looking over your shoulder and fearing a relapse.

In the same vein, another thing to keep in mind is to stop pushing away people who are close to you because you are ashamed of how your body "looks." This behavior pushes you into lonely corners, a scenario proven to increase stress on your body which lead to further skin picking. Instead, treasure and nurture your support system so that they can understand and help you through the periods when you need all your will power and strength to fight this continuing battle.

Lastly, remember this: never be afraid of people's judgment when you attempt to seek help. Thanks to society-imposed stigma on those who seek psychological help, many patients put off getting professional help, allowing the disease to escalate and take a firm hold. Due to such an environment, there are plenty of people who would rather self-help and self-medicate in an effort to solve the problem rather than approach a psychologist. Well, if it's a matter of pride, I can understand—you wish to give your own strength a shot before you seek help from another person, even a professionally-trained one. However, I strongly urge you to know your limits, and make the right decision before you become just another unreported statistic.

Finally, I'd like to thank you for purchasing this book! If you found it helpful, I'd greatly appreciate it if you'd take a moment to leave a review on Amazon. Thank you!

Made in the USA
Middletown, DE
23 March 2022